A FINANCIAL GUIDE FOR SMALL BUSINESS

G W Johnson

ISBN-13: 9781492158400
ISBN-10: 1492158402
Library of Congress Control Number: 2013915464
CreateSpace Independent Publishing Platform
North Charleston, South Carolina

ABOUT THE AUTHOR

G. W. Johnson has an accounting degree from the University of Arkansas and holds a CPA Certificate issued by the state of Arkansas currently classified as held in retirement status.

He is a former corporate controller and chief accounting officer for a Fortune 200 company. During the twenty-five years he spent with that company, he was involved in twenty-three acquisitions and saw the company grow from seventy million dollars in revenue to approximately seven billion. During one ten-year period before his retirement in 1996, the company was the third-best in the United States in terms of stock-price appreciation. The company experienced twenty-four record quarters in a row during the last years of his involvement. Mr. Johnson is a firm believer in providing management with timely, targeted information and the tools to control key aspects of a business.

After retiring from the Fortune 200 company, he was involved in a number of consulting projects lasting from days to as much as eight months. These projects were largely solicited by key executives, friends, and associates who knew him from his past career and who knew his skill and expertise.

He has served as a CEO for a small corporation that operated twelve retail stores in three states. He served in that capacity until the corporation found its financial footing and was attractive to a buyer. Subsequently, he has served as chief financial officer for two small businesses.

His most recent position, the one immediately prior to his last retirement, was as chief financial officer for a company that operated several nursing homes in two states. The company was on the doorstep of bankruptcy, with the imminent prospect of having certain assets seized by creditors, having assets delivered to the state commissioner of lands for failure to pay real estate and property taxes, and having the IRS place liens on the business for failure to pay payroll taxes. It was a truly desperate situation. Mr. Johnson was able to retire from this last position with all company taxes paid and current, all account payable within payment terms, significant amounts of long-term debt retired through the sale of certain assets, interest expense significantly reduced, and the company issuing profitable audited financial statements. All of this was accomplished within the span of two and a half years. The company continues to operate profitably using a concise set of operating and financial goals and a daily and weekly performance report tool constructed by Mr. Johnson that pinpoints on a timely basis how its facilities are operating and the direction of their financial trends.

The majority of Mr. Johnson's consulting work or employment positions subsequent to his position with the Fortune 200 company have been "rescue" projects. The results are a list of satisfied owners and investors.

INTRODUCTION

At times in the past, I have searched for easy solutions to a project problem or some hurdle I was facing. I wanted someone to provide me with a road map for the work I was encountering, someone who had blazed the trail before and was willing to share his or her experience and solutions. Most times, the material was not available or it was just plainly lacking in substance. So, generally, I created what I wanted, using my own experience.

This book is a brief guide for small-business financial managers who want a jump start for improving the financial condition of their company. Usually, such managers are busy, pressured individuals. If I were in their shoes, and I have been, I would want something that was easy to read and understand. I would want the material to be thought-provoking with some substance, and I would want it to have a real-world ring to it. I would want the material to get to the point quickly. In addition, I would want some templates to get me started.

The following chapters deal with areas that impact the financial success of small businesses. Although a good many areas are covered, the most substantive areas of this guide deal with **CREATING A PURCHASING MANUAL** to control the spending habits of a company, **CREATING WEEKLY REPORTS** to stay on top of the profitability trends of a company, along with **TEMPLATES** and **FORMS** that are easy to use and modify. However, do not discount the other areas of the guide. There are valuable pieces of wisdom in the guide, all of which are the result of a lifetime of varied experiences. If you only need a guide for creating a purchasing manual and the templates to get you started, the material in this guide is worth the price.

one

Creating A Purchasing Manual

THE BASICS

Don't Have Time to Read the Entire Purchasing Manual Guide?

This approach to developing a company purchasing manual is designed to be quick and painless. If you want to skip the following narrative detailing considerations for managing the purchasing function and developing an effective purchasing manual, you have that choice. Open up the template and start changing the wording to match your particular company. The template is not terribly elaborate. It is, after all, meant to fit a small company.

Larger companies will undoubtedly build their own purchasing manual from scratch. They will form committees probably involving their purchasing group, the accounting and finance group, the operations group, and perhaps even the information technology group. By the time the manual is drafted and edited by all concerned, they will undoubtedly have more than one thousand man-hours in the project. The approach in this book is meant to eliminate the bulk of that work. The book and the template were written by someone who has been through the big-company approach and who has also written purchasing manuals for smaller companies where none was previously in place.

The template has been sized for a small corporation that has a purchasing function. If your company is not a corporation and your approach to purchasing does not involve a formal purchasing function, then you will have to scale the template back to fit your particular situation. However, you will have a detailed set of considerations with which to pick and choose. The Purchasing Manual Template provided separately with this guide is created in Microsoft Word while the associated Forms were created in Microsoft Excel. Both office software tools are common in any business environment and should facilitate easy edits and alterations to the base template and base forms.

The purchasing manual does not cover managing labor cost, which is covered in another area of this guide. Managing labor cost is a subject near and dear to my heart. Effective management of labor cost will make or break a company. Very little discussion is devoted to managing utility cost in the purchasing manual. However, that subject is covered in another area of this guide. Utility cost is generally an area ripe for effective management that can create a positive impact on a company. The subject of this manual is the purchasing function extended to cover all avenues where funds or wealth can leave the company, including such activities as sale of assets, travel and entertainment, credit card usage, and cell-phone usage.

OBJECTIVES OF DEVELPING A PURCHASING MANUAL

Why Is Managing Expenditures so Important?

Remember the old business saying, "You have to spend money to make money"? Well, it is true under the right circumstances. If you can identify an opportunity to generate revenue or substantially reduce operating cost through an expenditure of funds, then by all means you should endeavor to make that investment. However, most of a company's cash is spent through routine day-to-day operations of the company. A company that can effectively control its expenditures and eliminate waste has a distinct advantage. Every dollar saved through proper management falls directly to the bottom line. Even major expenditures for assets and repairs should be scrutinized to ensure that those expenditures are necessary and that they are cost-effective.

What Functions Should Be Covered in a Purchasing Manual?

I tend to think that every avenue where cash leaves the company should be covered by a set of guidelines. Otherwise you are open to different interpretations by associates as to how to conduct business. I also think you should seize the opportunity to convey the need to follow your company's policy as to business ethics, compliance with prevailing laws, and the proper recording of all transactions.

To Whom Should the Purchasing Manual Be Distributed?

Although you can write a beautiful purchasing manual, with all the right subject matter covered, it will be worthless unless the associates in your company who need the information actually read it and understand it. My recommendation is to not only have printed copies of the manual available but also to store a copy on a public-access drive on your company's server. The forms that facilitate this manual should also be stored on the public-access drive. By making this information available online, the quantity of stored paper hard copies can be reduced. All of the forms can be filled in from your computer and most of the forms have automatic supporting calculations. Never spend time manually entering information and making manual calculations if it can be avoided. I recommend that all company policies, guidelines, and forms be available online. Finally, every associate who engages in any function covered by the manual should have to sign a form stating that he or she has read and understood the manual. Those forms should be a part of the associate's personnel files. The signed form can be a valuable tool to prevent an associate from stating that he or she was never informed as to a certain guideline. The signed form can be useful in those unfortunate situations that may require a termination action or may involve some legal action, particularly against the company.

Can an Effective Purchasing Manual Convince Auditors that Your Company Has Effective Internal Control Procedures?

The answer is yes. If your company does not have a set of guidelines dealing with the purchasing function, you may be hard-pressed to convince your auditors that you are serious about internal control. Certainly, it is a must for those publicly traded companies dealing with the significant burden of Sarbanes-Oxley legislation.

(Excerpts from the Purchasing Manual Template)

01. OBJECTIVES

1.01   **Statement of Objectives**

    A. The objectives of these policies and procedures are to ensure that the funds of the Company are spent in accordance with Company guidelines and are duly authorized and transacted by individuals with proper Company authority as documented in this manual.

    B. Further, it is the objective of the Company that all expenditures should be made in the pursuit of improving the financial condition of the Company and the betterment of its shareholders. Therefore, every effort shall be made to justify the expenditure as necessary to currently operate the Company in a profitable manner or to improve future profitability.

    C. All transactions shall be documented and/or recorded in such a manner that the transactions are clearly identified, that they are supported by proper forms or other documentation, and that such recording corresponds with Generally Accepted Accounting Principles. Every effort shall be made to ensure that financial results are fairly stated in financial reports to shareholders, as well as the internal reports presented to management.

D. Implementing and precisely following a set of purchasing policies and procedures for both the physical act of purchasing as well as establishing an accurate and consistent manner of recording purchases for accounting purposes are absolutely essential for compliance with Sarbanes-Oxley legislation. Documenting that such practices are firmly in place and rigidly followed will provide assurance to the Company's auditors that proper internal controls are in place and that the financial results as presented to shareholders are fairly stated. Further, these policies and procedures lend assurances to the Company's CEO and vice president of finance that they can sign with confidence the audit representation letter that is part of the Sarbanes-Oxley legislation attesting to the Company's establishment of proper internal controls.

GENERAL PURCHASING POLICIES AND PROCEDURES

Who Should Be Allowed to Obligate Your Company for Purchasing Transactions?

The answer to this question basically depends upon the size of your company. In small companies with only a few employees, perhaps only the owner or one high-level manager may be designated to obligate the company and even approve the payments. In larger companies, it will not be practical for one person to be in control of all purchasing transactions or the payment approval process. Therefore, depending on the size of your company, a level of purchasing authority may need to be established for various levels of management. Also, part of the equation should be whether the requested purchase is something used routinely in the operation of your business. *You want to be able to facilitate the purchase of goods or services that are needed in the everyday operations without constantly jumping through hoops and frustrating your associates.* One of the worst things you can do is build so much bureaucracy into your business operations that you make them inefficient. In addition, turning a high-level manager into a constant paper shuffler is a poor use of his or her time and talents. Therefore, you will have to decide how far down the management chain you want to push the approval process.

The flip side of this delegation issue is, how do you maintain effective control over the expenditures that directly affect your bottom line? *You cannot structure a system that is too loose or devoid of oversight, or you will give away your profits.*

As a corporate controller for a Fortune 200 company, I once performed a due-diligence investigation prior to the acquisition of a small processor of cooked beef products in southeastern Texas. Actually, the acquisition question had already been decided at the CEO and vice president of operations level, but as was usually the case, senior management finally decided to let the accounting and finance troops have their turn. One of the small company's primary customers was the school lunch program of Texas. Southern folks love their chicken fried steak, and cream gravy. The gentleman who owned this little company managed to eke out between one million and three million dollars of pretax income per year. There were processing plants in two Texas cities, so the operation was not extremely small. What distinguished this company as I completed my investigation was the degree to which the owner controlled everything. This was a man who understood that if he controlled spending, he put money in his pocket. He controlled his purchases. Some of his beef came from South American countries. He controlled how much was spent on supplies and maintaining the machinery and equipment. Some of his cookers leaked a little smoke into the plant where people worked. Every week he sat with his payment-selection printout and the corresponding stack of vouchers and went through every payment. One could argue that he was taking time away from the important oversight of operations. However, what he did was squeeze a good income out of his company. I suspected when I saw the books and the operations that my company could turn that little acquisition into a losing proposition. When you are a giant corporation, you cannot fly under the OSHA radar with smoky cookers. When you ship products to a distribution center in the Midwest and then ship them back to Texas as part of a series of drop shipments instead of shipping directly from plant to customer, it is not a good thing. When you load up an operation with overhead in terms of additional purchasing functions or human resources functions, it is not always a good thing. When you fail to factor in the increased operating cost of sourcing raw materials from more "preferred" suppliers, it is certainly not a good thing.

If you try to solve the issue of effective control over purchasing by loading up on people for the purchasing function, you may make the mistake of wasting profits through excessive bureaucracy. The question of how much of a purchasing function you need must be weighed carefully. I might remind you that empire building is a natural occurrence as well as a curse in any company. I have seen it happen over and over. If you are a small company, I would recommend that you start with the premise that you can cover the purchasing function with the managers already in place (assisted by their support personnel). You can then start altering that premise slowly as you work through the rational of workload versus effective purchasing control. I would not put something in place just because that is the way it happens in other companies.

I recently served as a chief financial officer for a small company with seven facilities. Actually, when I walked in the door, it had fourteen facilities, but we systematically sold operations until we stabilized the financial condition of the company and rescued it from the absolute certainty of bankruptcy. We were in no condition to add any unnecessary operating cost. Therefore, we functioned without any formal purchasing department. However, there were strict controls put into place that helped with the purchasing function without adding cost. Operating supplies and services were provided by an approved list of vendors under a negotiated pricing structure. Any new vendor had to be approved by senior management before transactions were allowed. Any unusual or large purchase had to be approved by senior management. Administrators at each facility were held responsible for the proper receipt of goods and services and their signatures on payment documents were required.

The Purchasing Manual Template, provided separately, gives you one view of how to structure the approval process. It assumes a small company but one with considerable operations and people under management. *As stated previously, you can readily alter and mold the template to fit your company.*

How Do You Install a System of Requisitioning Goods and Services Without Making It a Bureaucratic Mess?

Separation of duties is always a good thing in establishing financial controls. Filling out a requisition form clearly documents a need for goods or services by the manager with responsibility for the effective use of those goods or services. When that requisition is delivered to someone with purchasing authority, it creates a separation of duties. The separation of those two functions helps to more tightly control expenditures and the proper use of working capital. The manager who requisitions something is expected to only requisition what he or she clearly needs. That manager does not have control over the vendor or the price. An organization may allow managers who requisition goods and services to check with several vendors for the lowest price and the appropriateness of goods or services and document that on the requisition form. However, *allowing a lower-level manager to have complete control over all aspects of purchasing is a dangerous thing*. The manager with purchasing authority is responsible for ensuring on behalf of the company that items requisitioned are appropriate in light of the operations of the business. Additionally, the approval manager must ensure that the company is always getting the best price. Further, the approval manager must weigh such factors as inventory levels for those items that will be used over time. *Tying up money in unnecessary inventories is a waste of working capital.*

Okay, so you have decided to install a system of requisitioning goods and services. How you install it will have a direct effect on the efficiency of your associates. I would recommend that your requisition form be installed on a public-assess drive on your network. It would then be available to all managers who are approved to requisition goods or services. The form should function as a "fill-in form," with footing and cross-footing automatically calculated. If it can be accomplished by your information technology resources, I would recommend an electronic signature for such documents. By having a safe electronic signature for select management associates, there would be no need to even print a paper copy of the requisition form. I have seen companies forego the electronic signature function and just type their name in the requestor field and e-mail it. The theory is that the purchasing manager sees the e-mail address of the sender and associates it with the name on the request document. While that can work, it somehow does not seem as foolproof as a protected electronic signature.

If you can accomplish an electronic world where the requisition form, the purchase order, the receiving report, and the invoice are all electronically tagged to a payment voucher, you have a perfect world. Most small companies will not be able to accomplish that, but paper copies in a voucher packet are still a viable method of documenting payments.

How Should You Control the Receiving Function?

The Purchasing Manual Template assumes that your company will be large enough to have some sort of Purchase Order System and a formal Receiving Function. If you are small enough that you want to take a packing slip from your vendor, have someone sign it and use it as a receiving document; it is your decision. Just remember that without some degree of separation of duties, you are putting a lot of trust in your associates.

This discussion presumes, as the template is structured, that you have a Purchase Order Function and a Receiving Function. Hopefully, you will have someone whom you trust to receive goods and services at the point of delivery, whether at a warehouse, facility location, or office location. A very efficient way of controlling the receiving function is to share all purchase orders for a particular receiving location with the receiving manager. The Open Purchase Order may have a quantity-received column as part of the form. He or she then has all open purchase orders pertaining to that location on the location computer. When a vendor delivers an order, the receiving manager can print the purchase order and document the items received as they are unloaded off the delivery vehicle. The receiving document should be keyed back into the computer and sent to the purchasing manager and the accounting department. What do you want to bet that the receiving function will evolve into the receiving manager's signing the delivery slip for the delivery driver and just going to the computer and keying in the delivery slip information? If you are agreeable to that, so be it. However, *someone needs to impress on the receiving associates that it is extremely important for the sake of the company to make sure what we receive is what we ordered.* There is a school of thought that the Open Purchase Orders (or Receiving Report Forms) should not contain any quantities. By doing that, the theory is that the receiving associate has to actually count the items received so that what is entered into the computer is strictly based on the count. I do not subscribe to that theory. I believe it is fine to put the quantities on the receiving document. It gives the receiving associate something to check against and makes the process quicker.

Any formal Purchase Order System or Receiving Function is greatly enhanced if there is a Purchase Order Number associated with every order and every delivery. *Every delivery slip needs to have the Purchase Order Number shown somewhere on the document.* You may have to invest some time in impressing that fact upon your vendors. They want your business and they will eventually comply.

How Do I Evaluate Requests for Capital Expenditures and Major Repairs?

Capital expenditures are expensive and some element of evaluation concerning the need and/or the return on the investment should always be a part of such decisions. *Capital expenditures are absolutely an investment in your company with the hope of a future benefit.* However, converting funds to equipment purchases or brick and mortar carries huge consequences and those consequences last for years. The effect is magnified when a company takes on debt to finance such expenditures. Yet, it is amazing how many companies fund such investments without any significant research and evaluation. Generally, those situations occur when the owner or a high-level senior manager becomes convinced, for whatever reason, that such expenditures are needed. Sometimes it is difficult to change the culture of a company. However, successful companies make smart decisions with their money and they develop discipline in their approach to such decisions.

Major repairs, while somewhat different in nature, should be evaluated in much the same manner as a capital expenditure. Major repairs might be an absolute necessity in order to keep your facilities running and they may be characterized as an emergency. Those situations are easy to identify and to justify. However, I believe all major expenditures should be documented and justified. Consistency is a good thing. Other major repairs may be more discretionary in nature. Your company may be able to postpone them in many cases. Such expenditures need to be evaluated for need and return on investment in the same manner as a capital expenditure. Indeed, some major repairs may turn out to be capital expenditures upon further evaluation.

A form is provided separately with this guide and titled Authority for Expenditure (AFE). *It is a form meant to force members of management at all levels to justify a capital expenditures or major repairs.* The AFE Form has a companion form titled Capital Expenditure Decision (CED). These two forms are not elaborate and they can be filled out rather easily. However, the CED asks for supporting schedules to be attached that will contain all the calculations necessary to support the numbers entered into the CED. It is my experience that such supporting schedules generally require the involvement of accounting associates. However, this approach attempts to make the process as easy as possible, which in turn helps to achieve compliance by busy managers. Hopefully, the simplified approach helps to eliminate some of the roadblocks that cause managers to fail to fully justify requests for major expenditures. Knowing that they can have a helping hand from the accounting department certainly helps in this process.

The forms are a scaled-down version of an approach I developed for a Fortune 200 company many years ago. This was a company that grew from sales of seventy million dollars to seven billion in the twenty-five years that I was part of the accounting management. The approach has been copied by other companies in the same industry. I once presented this approach at a meeting of my peers who were part of an association of accounting and finance managers involved with the same industry. Most of the managers were intrigued by the approach and the manner in which every company decision was documented and justified. However, one of the attendees objected, stating it was not elaborate enough and did not cover proposed expenditures at the detail level and depth needed to fully understand such proposals. He was a mathematician hired by a small competitor whose job it was to perform those evaluations. Now, I can agree with that gentleman on a theoretical basis. However, on a practical basis, my company would have had to hire an army of mathematicians to cover the flood of requests that were part of our organization. My senior management would have become frustrated with the slow process of wading through the requests and most likely would have thrown the baby out with the bath water. Life is sometimes a trade-off. You can hire a team of mathematicians to perform such evaluations or you can design a system that is likely to facilitate compliance by everyone. The important backstop to this approach is that every form is subject to evaluation by the accounting department. You can kick the forms back to the requestor for more information or the accounting department can alter the process with more calculations.

Why Are Asset Transfers Part of These Guidelines?

The tracking of fixed assets is essential. You made a substantial investment in those assets. You need to know that your assets are protected. If you have assets, then you must have an Asset Register. How accurate is your asset register? Do your operations associates remove assets without informing the accounting department? Do your operations associates transfer assets between facilities without informing the accounting department? I have known facility managers to create a "boneyard" where they store equipment that has been pulled out of service. I have seen situations where only the facility manager and the head of maintenance know what is happening to the investment in a facility's assets. Even out-of-service equipment can be valuable. The equipment may have been removed from a manufacturing or processing line because of an overall upgrade to the facility. Whatever the reason, there are times when out-of-service equipment can be sold for significant sums of money. How much control do you have over managers who may be tempted to profit from an undisclosed sale of your company's assets? How can you determine a return of assets from a certain operation if you do not have an accurate handle on the assets actually employed in that operation? Fixed assets are an investment. They also represent a considerable piece of your company's wealth. I recommend that you install procedures for tracking the disposal or transfer of assets whether through sale, trade-in, transfer to another location, or simply taking assets out of service. Accurate asset registers or out-of-service inventories are essential. I recommend that you provide a facility manager with his or her own copy of the Fixed Asset Register at least once, preferably twice, a year. I further recommend that you send a representative of the accounting department to the facility at least once a year to perform a walk-through audit of the items in the Fixed Asset Register. Undoubtedly, accounting will get some blowback from operations people concerning the lack of identifying descriptions and numbers contained in the register. Actually, all of that is a good thing. It forces some practicality and discipline into the accounting process of recording asset purchases.

In the separately provided forms that are included with the Purchasing Manual Template is an Asset Tracking Form (ATF). Like all forms included with the template, it is meant to be a convenient, online fill-in form. I recommend you consider using it or designing your own company asset tracking form.

I would recommend that you open up the accompanying Purchasing Manual Template and the forms and review the material as you study this guide. A quick review back and forth will give you a perspective of how all of this material may help you. Also, it will give you a perspective of how the material may be altered to exactly fit your situation.

Please review the General Purchasing Policies and Procedures section of the accompanying Purchasing Manual Template. Also, please review the forms as mentioned herein for a perspective of how you might adapt this material to your company.

SPECIAL CHECK REQUESTS

How Do You Control Those Requests for Expenditures That Fall Outside the Realm of a Requisition/Purchase Order?

Invariably, one of your senior managers or an owner is going to come to you or your accounts payable department and ask to have a check written for a certain amount to some individual or company without anything in the way of documentation. It's just the culture of a small company. The man has a reason for that expenditure and he wants the check created immediately.

Other times there may be time constraints or a demand for prepayment that just does not allow for setting up vendors, issuing purchase orders, etc. That is a situation that happens in any size of company.

In my capacity as corporate controller for a Fortune 200 company, I have had the CEO send a demand for a check written on a page out of a yellow "Big Chief" tablet. Guess what, the "Big Chief" got processed. At least it had his signature on it. I understand the philosophy of picking your battles.

One way to cover these situations is by creating a form that I call a Special Check Request. It is a form that attempts to detail the expenditure, including the reason for the expenditure, the payee, and the amount. It is important to get the signature of a senior manager on the form even if it ends up being the controller or chief financial officer. If you are lucky, you can slowly change the culture of your organization so that all your managers understand that it takes, at least, a Special Check Request to document every expenditure. I have had to have an accounts payable manager fill out the form with all the important information and take it to the requesting manager for his or her signature. I will emphasize again that the approval signature should be that of a senior-level manager. A company should not accept the signature of a lower-level manager who does not have an appropriate level of approval.

Please review the Special Check Request Policy contained in the accompanying Purchasing Manual Template. Note that a form for Special Check Requests is contained in the accompanying forms material. Altering the material to meet your specific needs is always an option.

TRAVEL AND ENTERTAINMENT POLICY

How Do You Prevent Travel and Entertainment from Becoming Subject to Abuse and Ultimately a Drain on Company Funds?

Every company needs a Travel and Entertainment Policy that clearly states what your company will consider for reimbursement and what it will not. In the absence of such a clear policy, abuse will invariably occur. Unfortunately, for a lot of associates, living it up on the company's dollar is a big temptation. If you are going to control wasteful expenditures, you will need to eliminate that temptation. Also, some associates will create travel opportunities for themselves that do not have an appropriate business purpose. Your policy and your reimbursement forms should force associates to document the business purpose.

A good policy and a good reimbursement form also give your accounts payable associates a road map for determining whether a claimed reimbursement is appropriate and therefore should be processed for payment. In addition, proper documentation is needed for your tax accountants and the IRS in case of an audit. Further, your policy should be aligned with IRS guidelines.

Perhaps your company already has a good T&E Reimbursement Form. However, a T&E Reimbursement Form is included in the package of forms that comes with these guidelines for your consideration. As with other such forms, it is meant to be stored on a public-access drive on your server. It is an online "fill-in" form that performs footing and cross-footing. In addition, it will calculate the mileage reimbursement based on your company's stated mileage reimbursement amount. These features save time and frustration as well as promote accuracy in the documentation process. If you are having your people fill out your T&E Reimbursement Form in a completely manual format, you may want to consider a step forward.

Please review the Travel and Entertainment Policy contained in the accompanying Purchasing Policy Template. It contains some good points for consideration. Undoubtedly, you will want to alter it to suit the situations in your company.

PETTY CASH POLICY

Are You Handling the Petty Cash Function in the Most Efficient Manner?

While the loss is generally not large, Petty Cash is one of the most prevalent ways in which funds are misappropriated. Generally, Petty Cash funds have a tendency to become forgotten in the operation of a business.

To properly control Petty Cash, you need to have one person designated to be in charge of the cash box, cash drawer, or whatever repository is used. *You should not allow people to help themselves to funds, even if they bring an appropriate receipt for reimbursement. The person in charge should be aware that he or she is held responsible for the contents of the Petty Cash fund.* To further emphasize this point, any reimbursement of the fund should be in the form of a check made out in the name of that person as Petty Cashier. Cashing the check will be his or her responsibility.

I am a firm believer in requiring a complete reconciliation of the Petty Cash fund every time a request is made for reimbursement. There is a Petty Cash Reimbursement Form provided with the forms package as part of these Purchasing Manual guidelines. This form forces the Petty Cashier to reconcile the receipts attached for reimbursement (as well as recording in the ledger) and the remaining cash in the fund to the approved total amount of the Petty Cash fund. Clearly, any cash over or short will be documented, which will require an explanation to the best of the Petty Cashier's ability. The form facilitates this process in an efficient manner. It is also a "fill-in" form meant to be stored on a public-access drive. It will make calculations, including the calculation of cash over or short. The Petty Cashier can enter every receipt in the cash box in a quick fashion, enter the cash remaining in the cash box, and allow the form to make all the calculations to complete the form. The form is then printed, signed, and dated and the receipts are attached. This Petty Cash Reimbursement Request is then submitted for processing.

It is always a good idea to periodically audit the contents of a Petty Cash fund. The larger the approved amount, the more frequent the audit. At any time, the amount of receipts in the fund plus the cash should equal the approved amount of the fund.

Please review the Petty Cash Policy contained in the accompanying Purchasing Manual Template. It covers some important aspects of controlling Petty Cash.

COMPANY CREDIT CARDS

What Are the Pitfalls to Avoid with Company Credit Cards?

Issuing credit cards to employees comes with some trepidation. However, when your company reaches a certain size and part of the business involves associates traveling on behalf of the company, then you will undoubtedly come to a point where issuing company credit cards makes sense.

As the principal accounting officer in a company with a large contingent of sales and marketing associates, I dealt with the horrors of credit cards issued in the name of the company and carried by associates. The individual statements would come to the corporate accounting department and then the accounts payable staff would begin the nightmare of trying to track down the receipts that should have been turned in by the individual associates. There was an enormous amount of wasted resources involved in that process. It became obvious that something had to change. We met with banking representatives and came up with an alternative. We issued the cards in the name of the associates. They were responsible for paying the credit card statement. If they wanted to be reimbursed, they had to turn in all the appropriate receipts. It was amazing how fast things changed. I am sure this arrangement is common business practice today, but thirty-five years ago, it was not.

If you are not issuing credit cards directly in the name of your associates, then I recommend you consider it. The part of this arrangement that you do not broadcast with the associates is that although the issuing bank will make a concentrated effort to collect from the individual associate, your company will probably be obligated to pay if all other efforts fail. You will want to keep the credit limit at a reasonable level and you may want to look at it on the basis of the associate's position within your company. *Also, it is imperative that you have an agreement with the issuing bank that certain types of transactions are blocked.* For instance, you will not allow purchases of jewelry.

Some companies have a separate reimbursement form for credit card purchases. The Purchasing Manual Template takes the position that all credit card expenditures will be documented on the standard T&E Reimbursement Form. Credit card receipts will be included as well as receipts for payments in cash. From the standpoint of associates, they just have to know that when they are reimbursed, credit card statements have to be paid.

Every company should have a checklist of things to do immediately when an associate is terminated. At the top of that list should be the cancellation of the associate's credit card.

Please review the Credit Card Policy contained in the accompanying Purchasing Manual Template. You may need to alter it to suit the circumstances of your company. However, it will give you a good starting point.

COMPANY CELL-PHONE POLICY

Do Your Associates Know Their Obligation when Issued a Company Cell Phone?

We live in a technologically advanced world. More and more company associates are using cell phones for company business. It is getting to the point when certain managers feel that they cannot function without the latest multifunction phone. Certainly, a lot of information can be transmitted on a timely basis, decisions can be made quickly, and an associate can always be included in vital communication processes. These devices undoubtedly make our business processes more nimble.

The flip side of this issue is that it is easier to divert company time to personal time. An associate can do anything from keeping track of the stock market to placing a wager in the blink of an eye. You want to make sure that the use of company cell phones for personal business by associates, especially on company time, is not condoned. Also, you want to make sure that they do not use company cell phones in a manner that creates a safety hazard.

As a chief financial officer for a small health-care company, I had an occasion to be traveling with my newly appointed CEO in a small rental vehicle. In addition to driving ninety miles per hour in a vehicle that felt like it was never intended to be driven at that speed, my CEO was holding his Blackberry and entering text messages. He had his hands at the top of the steering wheel holding his little device, with his thumbs working furiously. I did not feel safe and I communicated that to him. It was not something that endeared him to me, but sometimes safety has to be a priority.

Please review the Cell Phone Policy as stated in the accompanying Purchasing Manual Template. It covers some basics of a good cell-phone policy. However, you may decide that you need to alter it to suit your company's specific circumstances.

COMPANY ETHICS POLICY

Why Would You Include a Policy on Company Ethics in a Purchasing Manual?

The issue of ethics is prevalent in every element of the purchasing function. You want your associates to know that you expect them to conduct business in an ethical manner while keeping the company's interest in mind. Further, you want them to sign off on every aspect of the Purchasing Manual, including the Ethics Policy.

You want your people to comply with all laws, and you want them to know that conflicts of interest with the company will not be tolerated. Depending on your type of business, the Ethics Policy can be expanded and/or fine-tuned. Some companies will have a separate elaborate Ethics Policy. In any event, if you are required to deal with Sarbanes-Oxley legislation, you must have a clear policy dealing with company ethics.

Please review the accompanying Purchasing Manual Template and specifically the section on Company Ethics Policy. It is fairly extensive and in my mind it states some extremely important aspects of how your associates are to conduct business.

two

Weekly Management Report

THE CASE FOR WEEKLY REPORTING

How Are These Reports Going to Help Me Run My Business?

First of all, I do not expect these report templates to exactly fit your operation. The underlying concepts are the most important aspects of this guide. *If you are not monitoring your business on a weekly basis, you are missing a great opportunity*. Hopefully, one of these templates will provoke a thought process and provide a start to getting you on the road to a weekly report. If you have a working knowledge of Excel, these templates are easy to alter or expand. Just remember to save a copy of the original in case you need to start over.

I have always been a hands-on manager. I like to get my hands dirty. I like to get into the details of how a business operates and obtain a working knowledge of all aspects of the business. If you are a financial manager in a small business, I just believe you have to have a working knowledge of how things work. The frontline managers are a great source of knowledge. They know how the business operates. It has been my experience that if you want to know what is wrong with a business, just ask one of those managers. Generally, they will tell you. It is important to be a good listener.

On the other hand, managers tend to get in a rut. If they did something a certain way in the past, they generally want to do it the same way in the future. It is extremely important to develop effective operational targets. Once you develop those simple targets and build them into a weekly reporting system, it is important to get management "buy-in." It all starts at the top of the organization. If you do not get the support of senior management, your challenges are tremendous. Even when you get senior management support, it takes a while to change the culture of an organization. You have to be patient but persistent. If you are trying to get operational management, for instance, to focus on labor efficiency, you are going to have to take the target information contained in the weekly reports and emphasize the meaning of the numbers each and every week. If you have multiple facilities or departments doing essentially the same thing, a comparison report is a great tool. *People are competitive. If you emphasize how one facility or department is performing compared to others, it has an impact.*

I should mention that the weekly reporting process does not have to be all about controlling costs. There should be enough information in the report to allow you to track and report on revenue trends. Falling revenues should be an immediate management concern. Opportunities for increasing revenues should be emphasized. *The profitability of one revenue category compared to another should be emphasized.* Organizations should concentrate their efforts in areas that are the most profitable. It is not that uncommon for companies to have a product mix where 20 percent of the products make 80 percent of the profits. I have seen salespeople who try so hard to make the customer happy that they change product specs at the drop of a hat. This can lead to the creation of a product that has limited demand. Such products can create problems by shutting down production lines to gear up to run this limited-demand product and thus drive up production costs. *I have seen companies create incentive bonus plans for salespeople based solely on sales volume without regard to profitability. It is a ridiculous, potentially disastrous but fairly common approach.*

Financial management generally has to become the spearhead of this endeavor. Just keep working diligently and enlist the help of senior management whenever it is needed, and eventually you will see the change in the culture of your organization. When the weekly numbers translate to monthly profits, that is when the pride and satisfaction really sinks in.

Two templates are provided in order help you create a Daily/Weekly Performance Report. One is a template for a service company. The other template is designed for a small processing/manufacturing company. That template can be adapted for a retail company with a few changes. These templates are not meant to be the exact design for your company. They are meant to be a thought-providing example for your company that can be altered and molded for to fit your needs.

It is suggested that you open the template that relates to your company and review it as you read this guide.

What Function Does the Key Variables Tab Perform?

The first tab in this report template is the **Key Variables** tab. Information entered in this tab will drive many aspects of the report. You may decide to add to or modify the information in this tab to match your operations. Please note that if you do so, you will need to modify the report layouts and change the formulas appropriately.

The report is based on a weekly payroll cycle. The week starts on Sunday and ends on Saturday. If that is not the weekly business cycle for your company, you will need to change that setup. *Hopefully, your payroll cycle corresponds with your production cycle. If it does not, you need to seriously consider changing one or the other so that they correspond.* Otherwise, any efforts at an effective cost-accounting approach will be hampered. Each reporting week, you will need to change the payroll period start date in the Key Variables tab so that the correct dates will populate the template. For instance, in the template, a date of 08/15/10 was used as the start date. The Weekly Management Report automatically populated the report with all the days in the week and that resulted in a weekly totals column appropriately headed by the last day of the week.

All the fields to be keyed are marked in blue font. Please note that the spreadsheet report can protected in such a manner that only the cells to be regularly changed (or keyed) are available for keying information. The key information in this tab may not need to be updated frequently (other than the start date) but should be updated as often as the information materially changes. Certain information in the Key Variables tab can be obtained from your financial statements, either the previous annual financials or quarterly financials, as you prefer.

How Can I Collect and Effectively Use Daily and Weekly Labor Data?

You should be able to update the **Labor Stats** tab from your daily time clock reports. *Most time clock systems these days have decent reporting capabilities that can give you the hours and the dollars of labor (including overtime) for different departments or categories within your company.* Simply take these daily reports and key the information into the appropriate fields each day. Remember to account for vacation and holiday pay. If vacation and holiday pay are not readily available in your weekly time clock reports, you will need to develop a system for adding them either manually or from some other report. You may need to change the Labor Stats tab in order to collect labor information in a manner that corresponds with your operation. If you do, remember to change the Weekly Management Report layout as needed and to change the formulas appropriately.

How Do You Account for Production Data if You Are a Manufacturing Company?

The **Production & Inventory** tab provided with the manufacturing template is meant to collect your production stats each day along with your ending inventories. The approach outlined for the **Manufacturing Company Daily/Weekly Management Report** is designed for a small company that does not have all of its production systems computerized and does not have a sophisticated cost-accounting system tied to these capabilities. Most of the larger companies will have all of these activities fully computerized and will have a cost-accounting department controlling the production cost that is generated. If you are of sufficient size and you have the financial resources, then you should consider that approach.

In the Weekly Manufacturing Report, there are five major product categories provided. Undoubtedly, your company will have a different number of major product categories, which means you will have to modify the input information and the report. If you are proficient in Excel, it will not be difficult. If you try to provide information about each and every product you produce, a weekly report will no longer be a concise one-page report. I have been involved with reporting systems that reported weekly profitability on more than six thousand products. In order to make ultimate sense of the report, products had to be summarized upward into a) Minor Product Lines and b) Major Product Lines (ultimately, the one-page report on which senior management focused was constructed on the basis of Major Product Lines). This template endeavors to provide a one-page report by your top-level product groupings (or major product lines). Problems highlighted by the weekly report will require you to consult other reporting capabilities to properly put the specific problem under the microscope. *Hopefully, your company has some system for collecting production data and inventory data each day. If not, you are essentially flying blind in an area that is critical to your success.*

How Do You Account for Cost of Sales if You Are a Retail Company?

The **Cost of Sales** tab, assuming you alter the **Manufacturing Daily/ Weekly Management Report Template** accordingly to create a **Retail Daily/Weekly Management Report** template, will help you collect the purchased cost of products sold. *Hopefully, your company has computer capabilities in connection with your cash-register records that provide you not* *only with sales information but also the categories and quantities of products sold.* The approach I have outlined in this retail management report is a simplistic tool designed for a small retail company. Larger retail companies will have all this information in a sophisticated computer reporting system.

If you are a small retail company, you will have to calculate (or use reporting capabilities) and determine the average purchased cost for your major sales categories. In a past life when I was the CEO/vice president of finance for a small retail company that I helped rescue, I geared ledger accounts to capture the units and purchased cost of various types of products. By doing that, I had a fairly accurate average cost of each category both in terms of total dollars and cost per unit. Admittedly, if the mix of purchases changed materially, the average cost per unit of a broad category was affected.

Undoubtedly, you will need to modify the input tabs and the Retail Weekly Management Report to correspond with your organization. If you change the input layout, you will also have to modify the weekly report and change the formulas accordingly.

How Can the Sales Tab Help Me Collect Information for the Daily/Weekly Management Report if I Am a Retail Company or a Manufacturing Company?

The **Sales** tab collects daily information on units sold and sales dollars. If you are a manufacturing company or a retail company, hopefully, you have the reporting capability to collect such data by major product category. As mentioned in a previous section, if you are a retail company, hopefully you have the ability to collect sales date from cash-register reporting. If you are a manufacturing company, surely you have an invoicing system that can report sales activity by major product category each day.

As the data is collected daily, it will be entered into the Sales tab. By the end of the week, the Weekly Management Report should reflect the sales for the week.

How Do I Obtain Revenue Data if I Am a Service Company?

If you are a service company, you should know how much you charge on average for various types of services you perform. That billing information should be entered into the **Key Variables** tab by type of service. This is not a complicated approach. *There will be a tab that collects data on the number of people you serviced each day or on the number of times you performed a certain service. The formulas in the management report will take that data and calculate the daily and weekly revenue.* This is a simplistic approach generally geared for a small company. However, I have used this simple approach with great success in a small company that owned several nursing homes. With an estimate of revenue each week, along with labor costs and other estimated operating costs, we had a report that gave us not only the estimated weekly profit but also targeted operating efficiencies, such as labor compared to revenue. *We had the means to target which types of service activities that generated the most profits and we concentrated our energy in that direction.* None of our smaller competitors had this weekly tool. The financial condition of that small nursing home company improved dramatically.

What Function Does the Comments Tab Perform?

The Comments tab is provided just in case you want to save notes on the week for historical purposes. The information in that tab does not affect any other parts of the report.

How Does the Management Report Spreadsheet Work?

Once you enter the required information in the data-collection tabs marked in blue (and recorded in the cells marked in blue font), the Daily Management Report will automatically populate. The report is actually a combination of a daily and a weekly report. There is a significant amount of information contained in the report. *A primary focus of the report is managing labor cost. My recommendation is to set goals for what labor cost should be* in order to maintain the profitability of your company, to produce your products in a cost-effective manner, to staff your retail operation in an efficient manner, or to control the labor in your service company so that you efficiently take care of your clients but do not overspend. *Another major focus is a simple estimate of your weekly profitability.* Waiting a month and a half after the fact to generate monthly financial statements is simply too long to effectively manage a business. These reports should give senior management a quick feel for a developing trend and help them emphasize areas where improvement is needed on a timely basis

three

Controlling Utility Costs

Why Should You Pay Attention to Utility Costs?

In a substantial number of businesses, utility costs are a significant portion of the cost of goods sold or operating costs. Taking the initiative to reduce utility costs means increased profitability. *Every dollar saved through such an initiative falls directly to the bottom line.*

What Is the First Step in Controlling Utility Costs?

The first step is an analysis of how utility costs are affecting your company.

1. Research your general ledger and your utility bills.
2. Document how much you are spending by location, department, or process.
3. Attach the units of measure to all such expenditures, whether measured in a) kilowatt hours, b) gallons, or c) cubic feet or BTUs. From the water bill, include any penalties for discharge of pollutants into the wastewater system, typically expressed as BOD count.

4. Try to find operational statistics within your business that can be used as a divisor that will allow you to make some analytical decisions. Such operational statistics may be a) square feet of a location, b) head count of patients, c) units of output, etc. Divide them into your utility costs or usage amounts to determine a cost or usage per operational unit. *If you have more than one location or department, such statistical calculations may pinpoint abnormalities when compared side by side.* I have found water leaks and malfunctioning electrical timers using this simple unit-of-measure calculation.

5. It is useful to calculate the percentage of your total utility costs that are due to a) electricity, b) natural gas or propane, and c) water. Further, I recommend expressing your utility costs as a percentage of your revenue and as a percentage of your total operating costs. Once you perform these calculations, you have a good idea how utility costs are affecting your business.

The next step in controlling utility cost is formulating a plan of action that includes a reduction goal. Having analyzed the current impact of utility costs on your company, setting a goal of reducing utilities, for instance, by 10 percent can be easily translated into dollars of savings and thus dollars of additional profit. Seeing the savings expressed as dollars of additional profit always provided an incentive to me.

What Are the Approaches to Starting a Utility Initiative?

1. Build a team—include representatives from management or administration. Top-level commitment is paramount.
2. Plan and lay groundwork—set goals (saving 10 percent, for instance).
3. Create an action plan—determine realistic measures of controlling utility usage tailored to your industry and prioritize.
4. Look at current energy usage and costs—see the areas where small improvements translate to increased profitability.

5. Consult with utility companies—utility companies may have information about typical energy usage in our business, utility incentive programs, discount rates, and energy-efficient equipment.

6. Conduct an audit of your facilities' utility use—a walk-through is a simple low-tech place to start. Pay particular attention to people's habits and procedures that can be adopted to use utilities more effectively.

7. Stay in touch periodically with the utility team. Have periodic meetings during the initial stages of the initiative with the objective of receiving constructive feedback and verification of action.

INITIATIVES BY CATEGORY

HEATING

A. *Low-cost initiatives.*

1. Faucet aerators installed in restrooms to restrict excessive water flow help both water heating and water usage.

2. Low-flow showerheads installed in shower facilities help both water heating and water usage.

3. Consider lowering the temperature of hot water heaters. If not permanently, then perhaps maintenance personnel could be set up to change water temperatures depending on workday usage or weekend usage.

4. Lower water temperatures in conjunction with washing chemicals designed to clean at lower temperatures (in the case of businesses such as motels, hospitals, nursing homes, etc., where laundry is a significant function) might be a solution.

5. Insulation – look to see if insulation of pipes and fittings would reduce losses.

6. Look at insulating the water heaters.

7. Re-caulk windows and door frames.

8. Examine and replace worn weather stripping for doors or windows.

9. Reexamine gas contracts and consumption numbers with a gas company representative in an effort to catch any opportunities for improvement.

10. Cooling and heating zones—examine the zones in the facilities to determine if some zones are getting more unnecessary consumption than others. Explore ways to recalibrate the flow of energy.

B. *More expensive initiatives.*
1. Purchase energy-efficient hot water heaters.
2. Purchase energy-efficient heating units.
3. Purchase and install energy-efficient windows.
4. Purchase clothes washers that spin at higher cycles and use less energy for businesses where laundry is a significant function.
5. Purchase low-water-use dishwashing equipment for businesses where washing dishes is a significant function.
6. Consider added insulation in the ceiling.

The more costly initiatives should be analyzed to determine the cost of the initiative versus the reduction in gas usage to determine if the initiative results in a desirable return on investment or payback period.

ELECTRICITY

A. *Low-cost initiatives.*
1. Lighting—according to statistics, lighting is 31 percent of the electrical load in a commercial building. You should consider compact fluorescent lights as replacements when bulbs burn out. They use 25 percent of the electricity used by incandescent lights and last up to ten times as long. You need to research the most cost-effective way to purchase compact fluorescents. Discount stores are always a consideration, but some electrical

supply houses will give you a substantial discount if they think they will be the supplier of choice.

2. Turn off lights, appliances, computer equipment (don't forget the monitors), and any other electrically powered device when not in use.

3. Caulking and weather stripping—you should look at opportunities to control lost heating and cooling and therefore conserve electricity. Caulking and weather stripping is such an opportunity.

4. Window coverings—bare windows tend to lose heating and cooling and therefore waste electricity. Consider window coverings that not only enhance the décor of the facility but also help with energy consumption.

5. Turn down the thermostat—during periods when high energy consumption is not needed, adjust the thermostat.

6. Establish a set time period for replacing filters in furnaces and the air conditioning system. Regular replacement of filters will save energy and reduce more expensive maintenance.

7. Look at some of the initiatives listed under Heating—heating, cooling, and electricity problems can be related.

8. Talk to electric company representatives about the electric bill and energy consumption. They may have suggestions. Also, there is no guarantee that the rates are set correctly. It is more common than you might think for a knowledgeable person to obtain a change in utility company rates.

B. *More expensive initiatives.*

1. Electronic ballasts—changing the ballasts in overhead fluorescent lighting to electronic energy-efficient ballasts can affect efficiency by up to 25 percent. However, along with the ballasts, you would undoubtedly have to replace fluorescent bulbs to be compatible.

2. Newer more energy-efficient cooking equipment and water heaters for certain businesses are always an option. Depending upon costs, return on investment (ROI) calculations, and

cash-flow needs, you may not want to consider those options unless forced to consider a replacement.

3. Examine the electrical drawdowns for motors and equipment used in your operations. Manufacturers should be able to provide information for their products. Whether you replace such equipment with more energy-efficient models, it is always interesting to compare your present situation with what is available and what the operating advantage might be. It is a simple step from that point to determining the ROI and payback for replacement. Then the decision process concerns cash flow, cash reserves, and competing opportunities for your capital expenditures.

4. Consider adding more insulation. Experts estimate that as much as 25 percent of your energy usage escapes through the ceiling. For facilities that have attic space where adding more insulation is an easier option, this may be quite viable. For facilities where the insulation is blown onto the ceiling and possibly hidden by drop-down ceiling tiles, this may be a more daunting project. Interrupting operations and causing down time is a serious consideration. A famous manufacturer of pianos used to have a mandatory two-week vacation for all employees in the middle of the summer. They used that two-week period for major maintenance to machinery and facilities. Changing the culture of an organization so drastically is generally not an option for most businesses. However, building inventories leading up to a maintenance shutdown and selling out of inventory levels might be an option.

5. Consider installing electronic thermostats that automatically control the temperature based on a programmable setting. This may not be terribly expensive depending on brands and suppliers.

The more costly initiatives should be analyzed to determine the cost of the initiative versus the reduction in electricity usage to determine if the initiative results in a desirable return on investment or payback period. While serving as the CEO of a retail chain, I realized that the lighting for the stores was a major expense. I converted several stores to energy-efficient ballasts and bulbs. My calculations showed that there was a definite return on investment. An unexpected benefit was that the stores looked better. They had a much warmer feel and a more pleasant atmosphere. However, there was a considerable amount of expense associated with these conversions and the length of time to recover the cost was as much as three years. Therefore, you will have to consider cash flow in such projects and whether you have the cash reserves to undertake them.

WATER

A. *Low-cost initiatives.*
1. The toilet—the toilet is a point where a considerable amount of water is wasted. *A traditional toilet uses eighteen liters per cycle.* If each person flushes the toilet four times per day, that translates to thirty thousand liters of fresh water per person per year. Some common solutions are:
   - Stop using the toilet as a wastebasket and flushing unnecessarily.
   - Check to see if your toilet is losing water by pouring a few drops of food coloring into the tank. If the water in the bowl becomes colored after a few minutes that means there is a leak, and that can use up to 200,000 liters per year or one thousand gallons per month.
   - Consider changing the flapper and older toilet components to more modern and efficient flushers (ones that can control the level of water in the tank). Consider lowering the flush usage from eighteen liters to nine liters. That is a saving of 50 percent over time.
   - If your toilet was installed before 1992, reduce the amount of water used by inserting a displacement device in the tank. Plastic water bottles filled with sand and water will suffice. (Do not use a brick).

2. Showers and baths—*after the toilet, showers and baths tend to use the most water.* Showers can consume between fifteen and twenty liters per minute. A ten-minute shower can consume 200 liters. Approximately seventy-five liters are needed to fill a standard bathtub. Some common solutions are:

   - If your shower fills a one-gallon bucket in less than twenty seconds, buy a low-flow showerhead. Such showerheads can save about half the amount of water without sacrificing comfort. One low-flow showerhead saves 750 gallons per month.
   - Choose showerheads with start/stop buttons. This allows for stopping the water while you soap up or apply shampoo. When turned back on, it has the same pressure and water temperature.

3. Water taps—traditional taps have a flow of 13.5 liters per minute, which is generally twice as much as needed. Solutions are:

   - Get in the habit of turning the tap off when not needed.
   - Install a low-flow faucet aerator that can cut water usage in half. Approximately six liters per minute are enough in the bathroom and between six and nine liters per minute are enough in the kitchen.

4. Washers and dishwashers—these machines use a considerable amount of water. Solutions are:

   - Wash full loads only.
   - Check with the water company to see if it has ideas or solutions. Ask for a full examination and explanation of the water bill. Ask if the company offers rebates to install water-efficient and energy-efficient washing machines.

5. Leaks—a drop of water per second can waste ten thousand liters of water per year. Solutions are:

   - Check for leaks and repair. A plumber or someone with plumbing experience could help. *If you turn off the water valves and the meter still runs, you have a leak somewhere.*

6. Outdoors—
   - Use a broom instead of a hose to clean your sidewalks and driveways.
   - Check outdoor faucets for leaks. Repair when necessary.
   - Use drip irrigation for shrubs and trees to apply water to the roots where it is needed. Only water when absolutely necessary. This should be done early in the morning to prevent evaporation. Water deeply but less frequently. Two times per week is sufficient when done properly.
   - If your business has a sprinkler system for the lawn, make sure it's on a separate meter to avoid sewer fees.
   - Do not cut grass below three inches. A higher cut encourages grass roots to grow deeper, shades the root system, and holds soil moisture.

B. *More expensive initiatives.*
1. For businesses where dishwashing and laundry are a significant function, consider replacing washers and dishwashing machines with water-saving models. If not immediately, then consider such equipment when it is time to replace the old equipment.
2. If you have a business that uses a significant amount of water in the operation, you may want to consider using some engineering expertise to determine how you can make your operation more efficient. However, I would always start with the utility company.
3. If your operation discharges pollutants into the wastewater system, you are undoubtedly at risk for surcharges from your utility company. You may want to consider some sort of pretreatment equipment. Depending upon a cost benefit analysis, you may find such equipment to be money well spent. Wastewater surcharges can be terribly expensive.

four

Revenue Generation

As a Member of the Financial Team, Can You Impact the Success of the Sales and Marketing Effort?

Everyone knows that the lifeblood of any business is a reliable revenue stream. It is absolutely critical to continually evaluate that revenue stream. *As an accounting professional, you can design reporting systems that make the decisions of senior management concerning revenue generation and profitability much easier.*

Do You Have Any Influence on the Sales and Marketing Team?

If you are an organization dependent upon a sales staff, talented people make a significant difference in driving revenue. I do not claim that as a new revelation, just a fact to begin the discussion of other points. Hiring the right people is critical. Compensation is very important. I am a believer in incentives. However, you need to be very careful about the incentive structure. Basing a sales incentive structure solely on the creation of sales volume is not always a good thing. I have seen such incentive programs actually have a negative effect on profits.

Sometimes salespeople, in the quest for additional sales volume, will promise the delivery of slightly different products that disrupt the processing function. *All new products should be thoroughly evaluated for potential demand and profitability.* Sometimes salespeople go after the easy sale in the quest for sales volume and ignore other products. The result can be a buildup of old products in inventory. People sometimes do not realize the effect of interest expense incurred on working capital that is not being turned properly. I have been known to be critical of some of the behavior patterns of salespeople. However, I appreciate a good sales staff. I have been in organizations where salespeople earned significantly more than I did. As long as I can see a significant positive impact on the revenue stream and on the organization's profitability, I can justify higher pay scales for a salesperson. *Again, the most important thing is that an effective, motivated sales function is the lifeblood of the business. Just do the math and see if the benefit justifies the cost.*

Does the Sales Staff Need to Be Evaluated in Conjunction with the Production Staff?

It is a mistake not to marry the sales staff with the production staff. Profitability is the bedrock of such a marriage. At least a piece of your incentive programs should reflect that fact. I have seen organizations give incentives to production people to run production lines with extreme efficiency without regard to the possible effect on profitability. Unmonitored, production people may run products that increase their efficiency ratings but build up inventories with products that do not turn over appropriately. An inventory system that monitors Days Sales in Inventory (DSI) is extremely important. DSI is one of those operational targets that should become one of several measures of the marriage between sales and production. There is no law that says you can only have one incentive element. Construct the incentive programs that ensure profitability in your organization.

What Are Some Important Considerations for a Retail Company?

If you are a retail organization, you had better pay attention to the details of store operation. The store needs to be clean, the merchandise well displayed, the signage should create a positive message, and people should be friendly, helpful, and courteous. Let me emphasize this last point. *It does not cost your organization a dime for the people to be friendly and courteous.* I was once the CEO of a small retail chain with twelve stores. I was hired to rescue this drowning little company. I made anonymous visits to the stores. Nothing takes the place of actually visiting retail stores. On one of my visits, a young man at a checkout counter was so rude and made such a bad impression, I was beside myself with anger. That young man was, in my mind, actually making an effort to drive customers away.

I think it is a good idea to have quarterly meetings with store management. It is a great opportunity to promote company spirit as well as educate and train. There are excellent training materials available that teach how to deal with an angry customer. You can seize the opportunity to teach those individuals about the relationships between revenue generation and operating efficiencies. Make such training simple and easy to understand. Play games where everyone has to participate. If you pay attention to those individuals, I believe they will end up being rejuvenated and more effective. Quarterly meetings are a good time to share ideas and management approaches between managers. It is also a good time to evaluate management skills and attitude. *Listen to your people.* You can learn a lot. I was able to determine which managers had an aptitude for higher management and which individuals had the right approach to managing a store and dealing with customers. One such individual became the organization's training manager who was especially valuable in training new store managers. Another individual eventually became the vice president of operations for the company.

Another very important piece of advice is to create a *Weekly Performance Report*. I am a big advocate of reports that measure labor efficiency and show a projection of weekly profits. Timely information is critical to fixing problems and monitoring trends. It gives you a timely perspective of the impact of a new product release. Develop your weekly report in a manner that shows estimated profitability of major product groups. *Focus on product groups that are successful and can be expanded.* One of my former CEOs had a folksy manner and one of his favorite homilies for successful product lines was to: "Let that dog have pups." Product lines that are struggling need to be analyzed. *What is the sales volume and can it be increased in some manner?* Involvement in strategy sessions by key management is critical. *Do you have an approach to adding new potentially successful products to the pipeline?* You have to stay up with competition. The same folksy CEO used to say that "*if you are not moving forward, you are moving backwards.*" I would hasten to warn you that many successful companies have made the mistake of trying to expand too rapidly. So, be careful about blindly charging ahead. Committing capital and resources to new opportunities needs be carefully evaluated. The consequences for not carefully doing your homework can be disastrous.

On the other hand, if you have a product line that is dragging down the entire business with no prospect of improving, have the courage to kill it. Jack Welch, the former CEO of General Electric, positively impacted General Electric by eliminating unprofitable product lines or product lines that were not among the national leaders.

Can You Help a Retail Business by Developing the Correct Incentive Plan?

Create an incentive plan for your key managers. I say key managers because if you influence those people, they will influence the people under them. A quarterly bonus based on store profitability is a good incentive option. A weekly bonus for labor efficiency, compared to revenue, is a timely way to influence labor costs. It has been my experience that it does not take a lot of bonus money to make this work. I was surprised to see how this worked. Managers who see the opportunity to earn just a little more money will make the effort when laying out their staff requirements compared to their anticipated customer traffic.

What Are Some Important Considerations for a Manufacturing or Processing Company?

Probably the most important consideration is concentrating on products that can be sold profitably. If you have gotten to the point of actually running a manufacturing or processing company, you have probably crossed that bridge.

Having some sort of cost-accounting system is imperative. If you have people who can accurately calculate the cost of producing products on a weekly basis and add those costs to your inventory system, you are fortunate. If you do not have those capabilities, you should be striving to get there. There are ways to create a cost-accounting approach without tremendous resources. Just remember when you get to the end of your monthly accounting period and the costs you have applied to your products are distorting your cost of sales, you are doing something wrong.

It is very difficult to project a weekly estimate of profitability without some estimate of what the manufacturing costs were in a particular week. Of course, *a weekly profitability estimate must be coupled with your billing system to obtain the product sales for a particular week. It all starts with product revenue.* Creating a weekly estimate of profitability that is coupled with your billing system will allow you to analyze the estimated profitability of major product groups, subgroups, and even down to the individual product level if your cost-accounting system and inventory system can support it. If you are a manufacturing or processing company, I would strongly recommend that you need to be on a 52/53-week year. In other words, it is much easier to calculate your results on a set number of weeks in a month rather than on a calendar month. Labor is always a huge component of every business and payroll periods generally end on a Friday, Saturday, or Sunday. Your cost-accounting system and your accounting periods should be geared in the same manner.

Once you have the right accounting approach, it is much easier to analyze the profitability of your product groups and your individual products. As with a retail business, *focusing on profitable revenue generation is imperative.* If you have a winner in terms of a profitable product, you need to ride it. If you are draining your profitability with products that are losing money, you need to eliminate them. *Some sort of approach to product development is the lifeblood of future revenue generation.*

What Are Some Important Considerations for a Service Company?

A service company generally has a set list of services that it provides. A doctor's clinic may provide a list of services based on the qualifications of the doctors on staff. Such clinics are generally in competition with other such health-care facilities in the area. They may not be able to set prices at will because of limitations due to competition and reimbursement rates set by insurance companies, health management organizations, Medicare, and Medicaid. What they must do *is a) control the quality of care, thus limiting lawsuits and other quality-of-care problems, b) endeavor to provide courteous, prompt services to patients, and c) determine which services are the most profitable and maximize those services whenever possible.*

I once served as the chief financial officer for a nursing home company. The company had numerous facilities in two states. This company was a disaster that had suffered from poor management and was about one step from bankruptcy. Numerous steps were taken to improve the financial condition of the company, all of which were eventually successful. One of the things I did was *install a Weekly Performance Report and instill the eleventh commandment—"Thou shalt make a profit."*

One thing I made very clear was that *the company was not going to sacrifice patient care for profitability.* That would have been pure stupidity. When the new management team was installed, including me, the company was embroiled in a number of costly lawsuits concerning patient care. Those lawsuits required a significant provision on the books for legal expenses. Money and resources were being spent on attorneys and working with consultants. Three years later, the lawsuits were insignificant and legal expenses were minor. Nursing homes are constantly at risk for inspections from state departments of health and human services. Violations equate to fines and bad publicity. I constantly pounded the table on doing in-house mock inspections. I believe *performing your own in-house checks on the condition of your business much in the same manner as a health department or other regulating agency would, helps you stay at the top compared to your competition.*

The nursing home company's Weekly Performance Report showed the profitability of various types of care and the estimated revenue for that care. All the weekly financial information for both revenue and cost of operations was shown on a per-patient basis including labor. All the nursing homes were shown on a comparative basis each week and a critique was issued by me. I wanted to praise the good results as well as point out areas for improvement for each home administrator. *Competition and pride in oneself is a powerful thing.* I concentrated a continuing dialogue on the most profitable type of service and it paid big dividends. The most profitable types of service were actually recruited by the administrators and their staff from hospitals and other sources. Year-end bonuses were created based on both profitability and quality-of-care issues. This company soon pulled itself from the doorstep of bankruptcy and became quite successful.

All the elements of my management team's approach can be adapted to any service organization. The financial manager is logically a driving factor in changing the culture of your company.

five

Starting A New Business

You may have a great idea you want to develop into a business, or perhaps you have some great business experience that you intend to put to use in starting your own company. Perhaps you and some business associates are going to combine your talents into a start-up business. Most people start the process by developing a business plan. Actually, your lending institution may require you to develop a business plan before it will consider loaning you or your business associates money.

Is This a Guide for Starting a New Business?

The answer is no. This guide is based on the premise that you have already started that business or that you are part of the management of that small business. My goal is to help improve the management and financial efficiency of that existing small business, not to guide you through the start-up. There are plenty of guides to writing or developing a business plan. Some are absolutely lousy. I have some strong opinions about the starting up of new businesses and I will share a few of those opinions below. As a bonus for buying this guide, I have included a *Business Plan Template* that you can download. It is an actual business plan that I constructed for a client. It may not come close to fitting your situation. However, it contains some elements that I believe are *essential* to preparing a business plan. It also has financial statements and supporting schedules constructed in Excel that have embedded formulas. Change one element and the whole model changes. You will have to perform manual iterations with the cash balance on the Balance Sheet in order to make the Balance Sheet balance and the Cash Flow Statement presentation work. The check totals at the bottom of the Balance Sheet and the Cash Flow Statement help determine what the Cash balance should be. It is hard to solve simultaneous equations in Excel.

Further, once you get your business off the ground, you may find this guide to be very useful in building that business into a financial success.

Do You Understand the Pitfalls of Starting a New Business?

I will give you some advice. Most of the guides to writing a business plan cover projected financial statements for only the first year of the business. Perhaps that will get you by the lenders. They generally cover such basic financial statements as an income statement and a balance sheet in addition to the detailed projections of various business elements. If you take this simplistic approach, you may be fooling yourself. If I were starting a business from scratch, I would project two years of financial statements. The first year of any business is saddled with start-up expenses and the challenge of developing a consistent revenue stream. By the second year, your business should be beyond the start-up challenges and you should see a viable performing company—or you may reluctantly see a company that does not seem to have a future. You may need to hire competent accounting help in making these projections. I would absolutely insist upon *projected cash-flow statements*. So many new businesses fail because they do not have adequate capital. You should have cash-flow statements that will show realistically, without inflated optimism, the amount of cash you will need to provide the assets used in the business and to withstand losses incurred in the start-up phase. Part of those cash-flow statements will be the amount of contributed capital or borrowed capital needed. *If the cash-flow statements do not show a viable scenario, then you need to rethink your strategy.*

HOW DO I DOWNLOAD MY TEMPLATES?

Direct your web browser to:
www.ameri-pro.biz

You will need to enter a keyword in order to gain access to the Download Templates page

Your Keyword is:
success

Thank you for purchasing this guide. I sincerely hope you find it interesting and useful.

www.ingramcontent.com/pod-product-compliance
Lightning Source LLC
Chambersburg PA
CBHW071643170526
45166CB00003B/1406